an introduction to the eighteenth edition of the dewey decimal classification

PROGRAMMED TEXTS IN
LIBRARY AND INFORMATION SCIENCE
SERIES EDITOR C D BATTY

An introduction to colon classification
by C D Batty

An introduction to Sears list of subject headings
by Philip Corrigan

An introduction to UDC
by Jean M Perreault

Learn to use books and libraries
by T W Burrell

an introduction to the eighteenth edition of the dewey decimal classification

C D BATTY
BA FLA

LINNET BOOKS & CLIVE BINGLEY

FIRST PUBLISHED 1971 BY CLIVE BINGLEY LTD
THIS EDITION SIMULTANEOUSLY PUBLISHED IN THE USA
BY LINNET BOOKS, AN IMPRINT OF SHOE STRING PRESS INC,
995 SHERMAN AVENUE, HAMDEN,
CONNECTICUT 06514
PRINTED IN GREAT BRITAIN
0-208-01067-X

CORRIGENDA

Changes in the format of DC18 decided after this program had been checked with the final manuscript have resulted in some anomalies. In the *Introduction* to this book reference is made to 'two volumes'; DC18 is published in three volumes, containing prefatory matter and auxiliary tables, the schedules, and the index respectively. The location of the auxiliary tables in the first volume means that all references to them in this program by pagination should be altered. The correct list and pagination are as follows:

Table	1	115-122
	2	123-374
	3	375-394
	4	395-397
	5	398-406
	6	407-419
	7	420-439

As a result of further examination and testing of the program the following corrections should be made in the text:

Frame	24 line 11	for 594 read 549
	35 line 28	for 788.14 read 788.41
	42 line 14	for frame 57 read frame 58
	49 line 10	for frame 54 read frame 55
	11	for frame 53 read frame 54
	78 line 12	for frame 95 read frame 81
	85 line 19	for frame 92 read frame 89
	21	for frame 89 read frame 92
	100 line 7	for 026, 737 read 026.737
	126 line 2	for LITERATURE read FICTION
	133 line 8	for 820.08003 read 820.8003
	137 line 8	for adds -2 from Table 4 read adds -21 from Table 6
	17	for 491.41381 read 443.9181
	138 line 3	for LITERATURE read FICTION
	149 line 9	for frame 158 read frame 157
	151 line 21	for frame 158 read frame 157
	154 line 9	for frame 158 read frame 157

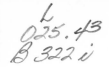

author's note

This book is one of a number of texts used in the research now in progress at the College of Librarianship Wales into the applicability of programmed learning techniques to education for librarianship. The purpose of these texts in the research programme is to test the suitability of the scrambled textbook in different forms for certain kinds of tuition; their purpose in the general educational effort of the college is to acquaint students with the mechanics of classification schemes outside the classroom, thus increasing the class time available for more valuable discussion and evaluation. In addition to this, the strictly practical instruction offered by these books is of direct relevance both to library in-service training and to the training of teacher librarians, neither of which command the time or facilities normally offered by full time professional education.

Few can be more aware than the author of the book's imperfections. In the ' author's note ' to the programmed text on the sixteenth edition of the *Dewey decimal classification* a hope was expressed that comment and criticism might improve future editions, and grateful thanks are due to those readers whose interest, sympathy and understanding helped to improve the text in revision. Inevitably, however, these revisions and the changes in DC17 and now in DC18 have necessitated a completely rewritten text, and the ever generous help and advice of colleagues and students alike is here gratefully acknowledged.

Particular thanks are due to Mr Benjamin A Custer, Editor of DC, and Mr Richard B Sealock of Forest Press, for their friendly encouragement and advice, and to them and to Mr A J Wells and Mr Joel Downing of the British National Bibliography for making available the typescript of DC18 before publication.

Those parts of the book directly reproduced from the eighteenth edition of the *Dewey decimal classification* are by permission of Forest Press Inc, owners of the copyright.

C D BATTY

HEAD OF THE DEPARTMENT OF INFORMATION RETRIEVAL STUDIES

COLLEGE OF LIBRARIANSHIP WALES

concept index

introduction

This book is intended to teach you the rudiments of practical classification with one classification scheme: Dewey's *Decimal classification*, eighteenth edition. It is not intended for use with any other classification scheme, even though the devices and methods discussed are of general validity.

The *Decimal classification* is a work in two volumes: the main schedules arranged in the order of the classes of the scheme, together with their numerical notation that gives the scheme its name; and the alphabetical subject index, called a 'relative index'. These volumes will be referred to respectively as *the schedules* and *the index*. The scheme will be referred to as DC.

You should have a copy of DC by you as you work through this book, and you should use it not only to solve the problems but also to check the examples and see how the scheme works.

This book is a 'scrambled textbook'; *ie* its pages are not read consecutively and indeed are not numbered as pages at all. Instead the lessons and problems are divided into *frames* and these are numbered boldly for easy reference. On the first page (frame 1) you will be given the first step of the course and at the bottom of the page you will find a question on the information you have been given. You will be offered a number of solutions to the question, only one of which is correct. If you choose the correct answer you will be directed to the next step of the course; if you choose the wrong answer you will be directed to an intermediate step where you will be shown your mistake and given more instruction. A further question will offer you the opportunity of proceeding to the next main step of the course. If at any time you wish to look again at a particular part of the programme you may do so by means of the *Concept index* facing this page.

Now turn to frame 1 and begin.

1 The basic operations for finding a class number for any subject are always the same: first consult the index for the required topic; then check the number given there in the schedules. In time you may come to know the schedules so well that you will be able to turn straight to the right area and look through the schedules for the number that you want, but until then, and even then if you are dealing with an unfamiliar subject, you will find the index useful for showing in what classes or disciplines your particular topic may appear so that you can select the right number.

You will find it useful when you use the index to look for the specific term rather than a general one. For instance, if you want to classify STARLINGS you will save yourself time and trouble if you look for that term in the index rather than for a general term like BIRDS, since you would then have to search through the schedules under BIRDS to find a number for STARLINGS. This is important when you are dealing with a phrase, because many people are tempted to turn phrases round unnecessarily. ELECTRICAL ENGINEERING is more specific as an entry than ENGINEERING, ELECTRICAL and saves you the trouble of looking all through the engineering section of the schedules.

We shall not use the index or the schedules yet. Instead, select which of the following terms you would look for in the index as the most specific

REINFORCED CONCRETE ROADS turn to frame 9
CONCRETE ROADS (REINFORCED) turn to frame 7
ROADS, REINFORCED CONCRETE turn to frame 2

2 No

You have chosen too general a term; you should have thought first of the *precise subject* contained in the phrase. ROADS, REINFORCED CONCRETE, for example, is only *generally* about ROADS, its particular concern is not even for CONCRETE ROADS, but for those of REINFORCED CONCRETE, and this is the term you should have chosen.

Now try this one
INTRODUCTION TO DIGITAL COMPUTERS turn to frame 5
DIGITAL COMPUTERS, AN INTRODUCTION turn to frame 9
COMPUTERS, DIGITAL, AN INTRODUCTION turn to frame 7

---

3 No

You are still choosing far too general a heading.

Go back to frame 1 and read the notes carefully—then work out the example again and see if you can understand why and how you should choose the *most precise term*. Then continue with the programme.

4 Not quite

You must not be put off by the way in which a subject is presented, or by its purpose, or by general terms applied to the particular subject.

In our example A BUSINESSMAN'S GUIDE TO TRAVEL IN SPAIN, the specific subject is SPAIN, whatever the mode of presentation. TRAVEL is a general term (travel *anywhere*) and you may waste time and effort searching in the classification scheme for a suitable way of limiting general terms like TRAVEL by the application of the particular field involved, like SPAIN. It would really be better to think first of SPAIN— the precise subject term. Still, you would have found the right class number if you had been using the schedules, since you could have read the notes under the general class number for TRAVEL and then found the specific place SPAIN.

Try another example
THE NURSE'S HANDBOOK OF OBSTETRICS
NURSE turn to frame 18
HANDBOOK turn to frame 12
OBSTETRICS turn to frame 16

5 No. You have made the same mistake again

Although in practice you may be successful in locating a precise class number for a term even after you have chosen a general term under which to look in the index and then the schedules, our concern here is to save time and trouble by looking first for the *precise term* that will give you a precise class number immediately. It is important to become used to thinking in this way as early as possible both for economy's sake and also because in this way you are beginning to think clearly about the subjects and to analyse them. This will be essential later on, with more complex subjects.

Try another example
THE LIBRARY IN THE UNIVERSITY turn to frame 3
UNIVERSITY LIBRARY turn to frame 9

---

6 Nearly

You have found the right general field and you have moved down the schedules to a much more specific heading, but it is one that could be divided still further to give the exact number for this precise topic that you will find listed there.

Now try another example
THE PHILOSOPHY OF INSTRUMENTALISM
144   turn to frame 25
144.5 turn to frame 27
140   turn to frame 21

7 No

You have avoided the most general of the possible terms, but you have still chosen a term more general than you need. You should be trying at this stage to think of the *most specific term* possible; you have ignored the adjective which would have given you a more specific term than just the noun.

In the example REINFORCED CONCRETE ROADS, the term ROADS is much too general and you realise this. CONCRETE ROADS is a more specific version, but it includes REINFORCED CONCRETE and it is this version that you should have had in mind.

Now try again
A TEXTBOOK ON GAS WELDING turn to frame 2
GAS WELDING, A TEXTBOOK turn to frame 9
WELDING, GAS—A TEXTBOOK turn to frame 5

---

8 No

You are trying to use the subject which is the original interest of the person for whom the book is written. This is only a slant or bias of the real subject of the work. What you want to find is the essential subject, not an aspect or intention.

Now try another
CHEMICAL FORMULAE FOR PHARMACOLOGISTS
PHARMACOLOGY turn to frame 17
CHEMISTRY turn to frame 14
FORMULAE turn to frame 11

Of course the language we write and speak can be ambiguous and confusing in its meaning and this is one of the reasons that we use classification at all—so that we can describe a book's subject in a clear and unique way that is easy to file and recognise. There are often words or phrases in the titles of books, or in the descriptions of their subjects, that have no real meaning or whose meaning is misleading, like the COMPLEAT ANGLER or NOTES TOWARDS A DEFINITION OF PHILOSOPHY (in three volumes).

These 'extra' words are of varying degrees of importance—some of them will describe aspects of the basic subject, or the form in which it is presented, like A DICTIONARY OF DOGS or MATHEMATICS FOR ENGINEERS, and we shall see later how we can use them in classifying. For now it is important to be able to decide what the basic subject is so that we can find it in the index and the schedules.

Which term in the following example best describes the specific subject concerned

A BUSINESSMAN'S GUIDE TO TRAVEL IN SPAIN

BUSINESS turn to frame 18
GUIDE turn to frame 12
TRAVEL turn to frame 4
SPAIN turn to frame 16

10 No

You have made the same mistake twice. This process of deciding on the *precise subject* is basic to classification and the use of a scheme. Although you may muddle through in practice with the help of a generous index and some knowledge of the schedules, there is no real substitute for accurate method, and sooner or later, in an unfamiliar subject, that is what you are going to need.

Now go back to frame 9 and read the notes carefully. Then work the problem again, and see this time if you can see how and why the subject is distinguished from its presentation.

---

11 No, you are wrong

This is the form in which the subject is presented and is not relevant at all to our present needs, though we may need to know what the form is later so that we can add something to the class number to describe the document more fully.

Now try again
AN ARCHITECT'S MATHEMATICAL COMPANION
ARCHITECTURE turn to frame 8
MATHEMATICS turn to frame 14
COMPANION turn to frame 17

12 No

You should not concern yourself with the *form* in which a work is presented, but with the *subject* of the work.

In our example of A BUSINESSMAN'S GUIDE TO TRAVEL IN SPAIN, the word GUIDE is far too vague a term to use as an index entry term, nor does it represent the subject of the work. Guides may be written not only to all places, but even to most subjects. In this example the subject (whatever the presentation) is SPAIN as a specific area of travel, and that is the term to have in mind. Still, it is true that in practice you could have found the right class number in DC by looking first for the general class TRAVEL and then following its instructions and schedules to the specific subdivision SPAIN.

Now try again

A COMPENDIUM OF MATHEMATICAL TABLES FOR THE ENGINEER

COMPENDIUM turn to frame 10
MATHEMATICS turn to frame 16
ENGINEER turn to frame 18

---

13 Not quite, though you are nearly right and would probably find the right class number if you were using the scheme

You have chosen the *general* subject field that contains the *specific* topic that concerns us here. The scheme would nearly always guide you very easily to the correct place anyway through the headings and notes of the schedules. But remember in future that you will help yourself to classify more easily and quickly if you analyse the subject accurately and recognise the specific topic with which you are concerned. You may then go on to work out the various aspects and limitations of the other ideas involved.

Now go on to frame 14.

14 Correct

Sometimes the title or description of the subject can guide you to the right place by setting the subject in the right context. Obviously ELECTRICAL ENGINEERING is one special kind of engineering belonging to the general field of ENGINEERING and is not ELECTRICITY IN PHYSICS, which is a theoretical discipline. Similarly THE GEOGRAPHY OF ALBANIA tells you that the subject is ALBANIA as a part of the discipline GEOGRAPHY rather than HISTORY or ECONOMICS.

Which is the specific topic in
THE CHEMISTRY OF RADIUM
RADIUM turn to frame 23
CHEMISTRY turn to frame 19

---

15 No

You were asked in what general field MEDICAL MICROBIOLOGY belonged. MICROBIOLOGY is the specific topic—MEDICINE is the term that tells you the general context.

Now go back to frame 14 and read the explanation again carefully. Then look at the question again with the examples in mind and continue with the programme.

This question of the basic subject of the book and the 'extra' ideas that may modify it is an important one. It would be impossible to deal with it fully in the middle of a course of this kind, but we shall come across it later on from a different point of view and you will learn more about it then in a practical way. For the time being keep a few general points in mind:

Never classify from the title of a book alone—nor even from the contents list if you are at all doubtful.

Eliminate the slant of a subject, the person for whom it was written, the form in which it is written, and except in special circumstances the place and period of the subject—you will then be nearer to defining the basic subject.

When you know what that basic subject is be sure you know also what general field or discipline it belongs to so that you will be able to find a number in the right context.

Now try another example. As before, without using DC yet, select which term you think is the specific and basic topic for which you would have to find a class number

A GEOLOGIST'S GUIDE TO THE CHEMISTRY OF SULPHUR

SULPHUR turn to frame 14
GEOLOGY turn to frame 8
GUIDES turn to frame 11
CHEMISTRY turn to frame 13

17 No

You are making the same mistake all over again. Go back to frame 16, read the explanation carefully and try the question again, working it on the lines of the examples you have seen.

---

18 No

The *bias* of a work (its presentation for a particular kind of reader) cannot describe its subject.

In the example of A BUSINESSMAN'S GUIDE TO TRAVEL IN SPAIN, the work is written for BUSINESSMEN, but businessmen are not the subject. The precise subject is SPAIN, as a specific area for travel. In practice you would find the right class number either by looking directly for SPAIN as a specific subdivision of TRAVEL, or for TRAVEL and specifying SPAIN according to the instructions or the schedules there.

Now try another
A STUDENT'S DICTIONARY OF MUSICAL TERMINOLOGY
DICTIONARY turn to frame 12
MUSIC turn to frame 16
STUDENT turn to frame 10

19 No, you are wrong

The presence of the word CHEMISTRY serves to tell you that RADIUM in this case does not belong to MEDICINE or NUCLEAR PHYSICS or PHOTOGRAPHY. It is the name of the general field—not the specific topic.

Now try another example.
In what general discipline does MEDICAL MICROBIOLOGY belong?
MEDICINE turn to frame 23
BIOLOGY turn to frame 15

---

20 No

You looked up GOLD and accepted a number in the field of GOLDSMITH-ING, which is entirely wrong here. Just because GOLD is mentioned specifically in that class is no reason to use it. The general field here is FOLKLORE, and although in 398.3 there is no specific mention of GOLD there is a class for MINERALS IN FOLKLORE that would include GOLD.

Now try
THE INTELLIGIBILITY OF SOUND
784.932 turn to frame 39
152.157 turn to frame 43
534.34 turn to frame 32

21 Not quite

You have found the number for the general field, but you have not persevered either in the index or in the schedules to find the exact number for the specific topic.

Try again
INSTALLING DISHWASHERS
696.12   turn to frame 6
696.184 turn to frame 27
696   turn to frame 25

---

22 No

You have confused the meaning of the word HORN and the number you have found is the number for MUSIC FOR HORN. You should always check the schedules carefully to see that you have the right meaning and context of the index term you are dealing with.

Now try this
INCORRIGIBILITY IN CHILD CRIME
364.36   turn to frame 38
155.453 turn to frame 28

23 Yes, you are right

Sometimes the subject of the book is not easily identified in the title or the contents, and you must always be ready to study the book further to find out just what the subject is. For instance, the subject of A HANDBOOK FOR WOMEN HATERS is WOMEN, not MISOGYNY. HANDBOOK is merely the form in which the work is cast and WOMEN HATERS are the ostensible readers—what they hope to read about (and, presumably, hate) is WOMEN.

In this programmed course we shall not be able to consult real books and instead we shall assume from now on that we have found what the subject is and what its aspects or intentions are, and see then how DC can provide us with a class number that represents all this clearly and accurately.

Now go on to frame 24.

---

24 Now we can begin to classify

Many subjects are easy; they occur only once in the whole scheme and they have an unmistakable class number. But whether or not you approach them through the index you must *always* check the number in the schedules. You should be able to tell if you have the right number by looking at any notes there may be at that heading and by looking at the numbers and the headings round about.

From now on in working the problems you should use DC18.

What is the correct number for
THE MINERALOGY OF JAMESONITE
594   turn to frame 21
549.3   turn to frame 6
549.35   turn to frame 27

25 No

You have now made the same mistake twice on this point.

Go back to frame 24 and read the lesson carefully. Then try the question again.

---

26 No

You have chosen much too general a place. Probably you looked up BOTANY or BOTANICAL SCIENCE in the index and used the number given there. You might have read through the schedules for 581 BOTANY (though they are much too long to make this a practicable way) and found the correct place: 583.55. It would have been better, and much easier, if you had looked in the index for the specific term SNEEZEWEED, for then you would have been directed easily to the number for ASTERALES—the botanical family that includes SNEEZEWEED.

Now try again
CLOSE-UP PHOTOGRAPHY
778   turn to frame 29
778.324 turn to frame 35

You will have noticed already that very often the index gives a second word or phrase after the entry term. In many cases this merely defines the general field to which the entry term belongs and confirms you in your choice. Frequently, however, a topic occurs in many different fields, as we suggested a few moments ago—for example LIGHTING occurs in BUILDING, ELECTRICAL ENGINEERING, ILLUMINATION ENGINEERING, PHOTOGRAPHY and several others. These scattered but related topics are called *distributed relatives* and it is the job of DC's Relative Index to show this relation and help us to distinguish the correct subject field to which our version of the entry term belongs by adding descriptive terms.

It is vital to use a class number in the correct main class; if, for instance, we had found a number for THE MINERALOGY OF JAMESONITE in LEAD GEOLOGY (where JAMESONITE belongs in its geological aspects) it would have been quite wrong. You must *always* check not only that your class number is accurate but also that it is appropriate and in the right general field of knowledge.

What is the correct number for
THE BOTANY OF SNEEZEWEED
635.93355 turn to frame 31
583.55   turn to frame 35
580   turn to frame 26

28 No

You have chosen the wrong number, either by not checking it in the schedules, or by not rephrasing the subject to the more useful JUVENILE DELINQUENTS.

Now go back to frame 35 and read the notes carefully. Then work the problem again.

---

29 Wrong

You are still thinking first of the *general* inclusive term. PHOTOGRAPHY is the general field containing among other kinds, CLOSE-UP PHOTOGRAPHY. You should have consulted the *index* under CLOSE-UP and you would have been led to the correct answer—778.324.

However, for future reference remember this. You can still find the correct precise placing even if you start with the general inclusive term, if, when you check the number in the *schedules*, you run through the subdivisions. If you have consulted the appropriate general term, the correct subdivision should then reveal itself.

Now go back to frame 27 and try again.

30 Wrong

You have confused the meaning of the word HORN, and the number you have found is the number for HORNS in the MANUFACTURE OF MUSICAL INSTRUMENTS. Though it is true that horns often have decorative work on them, the example here is intended to mean HORN as a material.

Now try this
INCORRIGIBILITY IN CHILD CRIME
364.36   turn to frame 38
155.453 turn to frame 28

---

31 No

You looked up SNEEZEWEED in the index and assumed that 635.93355 was as close a place as you were likely to find. But 635.9 is FLORI-CULTURE, not BOTANY. You should have looked under SNEEZEWEED itself, and then you would have learned the correct number 583.55 for ASTERALES (the botanical family that includes SNEEZEWEED).

Now try this
CLOSE-UP PHOTOGRAPHY
778   turn to frame 29
778.324 turn to frame 35

32 No

You have chosen a place in the wrong subject field. If you had looked up TONE, or TIMBRE, or even AUDIOLOGY, or if you had realised that the INTELLIGIBILITY OF SOUND deals basically with PERCEPTION and had scanned the relevant sections of PSYCHOLOGY, then you would have found the right answer: 152.157.

Study the example again to see why your choice of 534.34 was wrong, and then go on to frame 43.

---

33 No

You looked up GOLD and found a number in the general field of ECONOMIC GEOLOGY, which is quite wrong here. Just because GOLD is mentioned specifically in that class is no reason to use it. The general field here is FOLKLORE, and although in 398.3 there is no specific mention of GOLD there is a class for MINERALS IN FOLKLORE that would include GOLD.

Now try
THE INTELLIGIBILITY OF SOUND
784.932   turn to frame 39
152.157   turn to frame 43
534.34   turn to frame 32

34 No

You are still mistaken about the nature of *synthesis*. It is not the list of terms or aspects to be used, and it is not the prefabricated complex subject that sometimes finds its way into a classification scheme. It is simply the *combination of parts* of a classification scheme (in themselves probably simple ideas) to represent complex ideas.

Now turn back to frame 43 and read the lesson carefully before trying the question again.

The added term in the *index* entry can always be used in this way to help decide which place to choose.

Of course, it is rare to find a title or subject phrase that corresponds exactly with the entry term in the *index*; you must formulate your own before you begin to search. This is not difficult; the *index* usually lists synonyms, and even if at the first attempt you cannot find anything near your specific term, a little rephrasing will often produce a reasonable approximation. In any case, remember that you can always look up a number you recognise as representing a broader, more general topic and search in the *schedules* at that number for the specific place you require. *Index* entries printed in bold type are headings subdivided in the *schedules*.

Class headings and names in the *schedules* often have synonyms or explanations in brackets or in small type; these can be of great assistance in interpreting your subject. Notice also the presence of explanatory notes—often called ' scope notes '—which are intended primarily to define the range and limits of the subject, but often include terms and names, and may mention the one you have in mind. Always read these notes very carefully.

For example ANIMALS WITHOUT BACKBONES could give you trouble if you look up either ANIMALS or BACKBONES in the index, where DC lists class numbers for the relevant individual fields but without showing us anything directly helpful. What you must do is translate the phrase ANIMALS WITHOUT BACKBONES into the more scientific INVERTEBRATES, which can be found without trouble.

Which of the following numbers is correct for
DECORATIVE HORN CARVING

788.14   turn to frame 22
681.8184   turn to frame 30
789.913684 turn to frame 36
736.6   turn to frame 38

36 No

You have mistaken the meaning of the word HORN, and you cannot have checked the number you selected in the schedules. The meaning of the number you have chosen is RECORDINGS OF MUSIC FOR HORN! Always check the class number in the schedules.

Now go back to frame 35 and try the question again.

---

37 No

You looked up GOLD and accepted the number in the field of MINERALOGY which is entirely wrong here. Just because GOLD is mentioned specifically in that class is no reason to use it. The general field here is FOLKLORE, and although in 398.3 there is no specific mention of GOLD, there is a class for MINERALS IN FOLKLORE that would include GOLD.

Now try
THE INTELLIGIBILITY OF SOUND
784.932 turn to frame 39
152.157 turn to frame 43
534.34   turn to frame 32

Sometimes, in spite of all your efforts, you will fail to find either a relevant entry in the index, or a specific place in the correct main class in the scheme. This is because the subject you are concerned with lies beyond the development of the scheme—it is too specific. In this case you must find the closest general heading or class which would, if developed, include your subject. As we have already noticed, scope notes and explanations can be of great assistance in these cases.

For example 736.25 is the number for SAPPHIRES in the general field of PRECIOUS STONES. The MINERALOGY OF SAPPHIRES, however belongs to the field of MINERALOGY; sapphires are only one of a group of minerals of the HEMATITE GROUP, not all precious stones, and they must share a number with rubies, corundum and hematite. Indeed sapphires are not mentioned by that name in the schedules, but in spite of this we must place them in the correct main class. So for THE MINERALOGY OF SAPPHIRES, in spite of their specific listing in 736.25, the more general heading of 549.523 MINERALOGY OF THE HEMATIC GROUP OF OXIDES is the best.

Beware! Do not be led astray by the presence of the specific term you seek *in the wrong subject field*. As we have seen, it is most important to find a place in the correct main class, and it is no fault of yours (or the scheme for that matter) if one class has been developed to include one manifestation of a topic, when the class you are concerned with has not been developed sufficiently to name the topic you are trying to place.

Now choose a number for
GOLD IN FOLKLORE
398.3   turn to frame 44
398.365 turn to frame 43
549.23   turn to frame 37
739.22   turn to frame 20
553.41   turn to frame 33

39 No

You have chosen a place in the wrong subject field. If you had looked up TONE, or TIMBRE, or even AUDIOLOGY, or if you had realised that the INTELLIGIBILITY OF SOUND deals basically with PERCEPTION and had scanned the relevant sections of PSYCHOLOGY, then you would have found the right answer: 152.157.

Study the example again to see why your choice of 784.932 was wrong, and then go on to frame 43.

---

40 No

A list of common aspects or subdivisions for addition to an appropriate simple subject to make it complex is *not synthesis,* but the synthetic device that makes it possible. *Synthesis* is the process of joining the parts of the scheme together, of adding the terms from that list, and should be distinguished clearly from the list itself. *Synthesis* is the operation; the *synthetic device* is the apparatus with which the operation takes effect.

Which of these statements is correct?
Synthesis is the listing in a classification scheme of complex subjects with common aspects or forms of presentation. Turn to frame 34.
Synthesis is the combination of parts of a classification scheme to represent complex subjects. Turn to frame 47.

41 You are wrong

You have found the right number for both the class and the *standard subdivision,* but you have not put them together in the right order. The standard subdivision, as its name implies, is always a subdivision of something else; this is not surprising since it usually represents an aspect of the subject or the form in which it is presented. It can never stand first, or, of course, by itself; it must always come after a class number.

Now try this one
THE THEATRE MONTHLY
050.792   turn to frame 48
792.5   turn to frame 50
792.05   turn to frame 53
792—05 turn to frame 45

---

42 Wrong

You remember quite correctly that when we add a *standard subdivision* to a class number that already ends in 0 we must take away the surplus zeros, but you did not remember that one zero must be left to indicate that a common subdivision is being used. Otherwise the resulting number may be confused with a *subject subdivision* in the same class.

For example, to add —05 PERIODICALS to 610 MEDICINE deleting all zeros is to get 615, which is not the number for MEDICAL JOURNALS, but PHARMACOLOGY AND THERAPEUTICS—one of the subclasses of MEDICINE. The correct answer is 610.5.

Now try again. What is the number for
A HISTORY OF METAPHYSICS
119   turn to frame 57
110.09 turn to frame 60
110.9   turn to frame 52

Quite often a phrase that is not in the index will, by the structure of language itself, produce a term that does appear in the index, simply by reversing the order of words.

In spite of the warnings of the last lesson there are many subjects that cannot be named specifically in an index, or be given specific places in the schedules, but for which the scheme can provide exact class numbers. These are often complex subjects, where a simple subject is given a particular aspect, or is presented in a special way, or is even subdivided into classes belonging originally to another subject. These aspects, forms of presentation or subject subdivisions are often found to apply not to one subject only but to several or even all subjects.

Here are some examples: a HISTORY of SCIENCE; the ECONOMICS of FARMING; an ENCYCLOPEDIA of MUSIC; the WILD LIFE of SCOTLAND; the influence of TELEVISION on the CINEMA.

What many schemes do in such cases, DC among them, is to economise on the size of the printed scheme, and help the user, by printing commonly recurring aspects and subdivisions once only, with instructions on how to use them again when necessary. Combining elements of the scheme (and their class numbers) in this way to represent complex ideas is called *synthesis* and any list or arrangement that allows it is called a *synthetic device*.

Which of the following phrases best describes *synthesis*?

The presence of two or more ideas to make a complex subject. Turn to frame 46

A list of aspects or subdivisions to be added to a simple subject to make a complex one. Turn to frame 40

The combination of parts of a classification scheme to represent complex subjects. Turn to frame 47.

44 No

You are nearly right, but 398.3 is for *all* real subjects of FOLKLORE and is not specific enough. Certainly GOLD is not used in the index to guide you here (though MINERALS is) and in any case you should always read the whole of the class to make sure that you have the right place. MINERALS is the best heading that will also include GOLD.

Now try
THE INTELLIGIBILITY OF SOUND
784.932 turn to frame 39
152.157 turn to frame 43
534.34   turn to frame 32

---

45 No

You should not use the whole of the *standard subdivision* including the dash. That is to show you only that the standard subdivision should be added to a class number from the schedules. Always leave out the dash and add the rest of the standard subdivision as shown in the list.

Now try again
CASE STUDIES IN LIBRARY REFERENCE SERVICES
025.202552   turn to frame 41
025.52—0722 turn to frame 48
025.52722   turn to frame 50
025.520722   turn to frame 53

The presence of two or more ideas in a subject makes that subject a complex one and more difficult to classify. It would be a very large and complicated scheme that listed in order as many complex ideas as the scheme's originator could think of (though there are some that try!). Most schemes content themselves with listing fairly simple ideas (and there are quite enough of them) and arranging them in their groups or classes. But most schemes also recognise that complex subjects exist, and where possible they allow numbers for different simple subjects or ideas to be joined to make complex ones. It is this kind of joining that is called synthesis. The commonest kind of synthesis occurs when a group of ideas is found to be common to a large number of subjects. This group can be written down once and given special notation to allow it to be added to any of the appropriate subjects. An arrangement of this sort is called a *synthetic device*.

Which of these sentences is correct?

Synthesis is the listing in a classification scheme of complex subjects with common aspects or forms of presentation. Turn to frame 34.

Synthesis is the combination of parts of a classification scheme to represent complex subjects. Turn to frame 47.

One of the most frequent examples of recurrent aspects is the *form of presentation*. This can be both *physical,* as in the form of arrangement, like a dictionary, or concerned with the *approach to the subject,* as in its history. Form of presentation applies almost equally to all subjects, and a list of what DC calls *standard subdivisions* (our first *synthetic device*) is given at the beginning of the index volume: Table 1, on pages 2123-2134. These divisions can be added to any number in the scheme with a very few, clearly indicated exceptions. The dash is not included in the final class number; it shows merely that *standard subdivisions* must be used with a class number from the schedules. Otherwise they are added as they stand, so that the symbol 0, never used to represent a subject subdivision, indicates that the following digit shows the form of the work.

One of the standard subdivisions, —09 HISTORICAL AND GEOGRAPHICAL TREATMENT, can also be extended to give geographical subdivision and we shall see how to use this later. For the time being we shall concentrate on the standard subdivisions that show the form of presentation.

To give an example of their use: the standard subdivision which indicates the DICTIONARY FORM is —03 and the number for ELECTRICAL ENGINEERING is 621.3; A DICTIONARY OF ELECTRICAL ENGINEERING TERMS is therefore 621.303. Again, the standard subdivision —09 represents HISTORY AND LOCAL TREATMENT and PIRACY is 364.135. A HISTORY OF PIRACY is therefore 364.13509.

Now find the number for
THE THEORY AND PHILOSOPHY OF MATERIALS CONTROL

658.7—01 turn to frame 45
658.71   turn to frame 50
658.701   turn to frame 53
100.6587 turn to frame 41

48 No. You have made the same mistake twice

You may have to use *standard subdivisions* many times in classifying books and it is worth taking care now to get them right. All you have to do is to select a class number for the subject of the book and add to it the standard subdivision which represents its form. To do this you leave out the dash and add the standard subdivision as it stands including the o that shows that it is a standard subdivision and not one of the subject's own subdivisions.

Now go back to frame 47 and read the explanation again carefully. Then work the problem, keeping the examples and the explanation in mind.

---

49 No

Like the standard subdivisions the 'Areas' notation must be added to an existing class number and this is shown by the dash, which disappears when the area notation is used. WAGES IN FRANCE, for example, is made up of 331.29 HISTORICAL AND GEOGRAPHICAL TREAT-MENT OF WAGES and the area notation —44 FRANCE. Since the instruction at 331.29 says ' add "Areas " notation . . .' it is a simple matter to construct the number 331.2944—without the dash.

Now try again
SOIL AND SOIL CONSERVATION IN NORTH EASTERN INDIA
631.49541   turn to frame 54
631.49—541 turn to frame 53
631.499541 turn to frame 59

50 No

You have found the right numbers for both the class and the *standard subdivision*, but you have not put them together correctly. The 0 of the standard subdivision is an *indicator* to show what sort of subdivision is being used (*ie* not an ordinary subject subdivision) and it must therefore be retained.

PROGRAMMED INSTRUCTION (—077) IN STATISTICAL MATHEMATICS (519.5) is simply 519.5077.

Now try again
A HISTORY OF LITERARY FORGERIES
098.309   turn to frame 53
090.983   turn to frame 41
098.39   turn to frame 48
098.3—09 turn to frame 45

---

51 No

You have ignored the instruction that tells you:
    636.8001-636.8009 standard subdivisions
DC includes this instruction because places in 636.801-.809 are used for special subdivisions for the aspects of cats and their care. The answer should have been 636.8003.

Now remember in future to read and follow DC's instructions and notes.

Turn to frame 57.

52 Correct.

Now you have learned how to use standard subdivisions let us look at another table of common subdivisions also in volume 2 of DC—Table 2: AREAS. These are used to show division or limitation by place, *ie*, geographical subdivision: general kinds of geographical subdivision like land forms, oceans, etc, followed by specific continents and countries.

Almost any class may need geographical subdivision at some time, but in many classes place is one of the important kinds of subdivision and DC gives specific instructions on what to do.

In 367 GENERAL CLUBS, for instance, we find 367.91-.99 allocated to HISTORICAL AND GEOGRAPHICAL TREATMENT with the instruction

Add 'Areas' notation 1-9 from Table 2 to base number 367.9

All we have to do to find a number for CLUBS IN SWEDEN is to add the area notation for SWEDEN —485 to 367.9 to get 367.9485 CLUBS IN SWEDEN. Again, 526.32 SURVEY BENCH MARKS may be extended by an area table number like —415 IRELAND to give 526.32415 SURVEY BENCH MARKS IN IRELAND.

Now find one for yourself
WAGES IN FRANCE

331.2944   turn to frame 55
331.29—44 turn to frame 49
331.29944 turn to frame 59

53 Good

Sometimes, for one reason or another, DC will include a special instruction in a class to use more than one zero for *standard subdivisions*. There can be several reasons for this and we will come to them later. For now, you should remember that you can use standard subdivisions anywhere if DC has no special instruction, and that then you should use the single zero shown in the table of standard subdivisions, but that if DC has a special instruction to use more, then you must follow it.

What is the number for
A DICTIONARY OF CATS
636.803   turn to frame 51
636.8003   turn to frame 57

---

54 No

You have just made the same mistake twice and it is unlikely that you really understand the nature and use of area notation.

Table 2 gives a list of countries and places and some geographical features, so that the notation can be added on instruction wherever it is needed. At the moment we are thinking only of the cases where DC gives a specific instruction to use *any* area notation, and in these cases all you have to do is to write the digits of the area notation after the class number concerned.

Now turn to frame 52 again, read the explanation carefully and try the question again.

55 Good

You found the correct class number in the schedules and you added the correct area table number according to the instructions (without the dash, of course) to get the right answer. Now try another one, this time using one of the early, more general geographical divisions.

SCHOOL ENROLMENT IN RURAL AREAS

371.2191734   turn to frame 67
371.211734   turn to frame 61
371.219—1734 turn to frame 56

---

56 No

You have used the right area notation but you have chosen to keep the dash shown in the area notation. This is only to show that area notation cannot stand alone but must be added to an existing class number. In use it disappears.

Now try again

URBAN FOLKSONG

784.41732   turn to frame 61
784.491732   turn to frame 67
784.49—1732 turn to frame 64

One exception to the simple addition of *standard subdivisions* to a class number in the way that we have seen already arises when that number already ends in o. In many cases of this kind you will find that DC gives careful instructions and examples on the use of *standard subdivisions*. Always look for notes at any class number you choose and read them carefully. But sometimes there is no instruction and then you must work out the compound number for yourself. Unless there is a contrary instruction there is never any need to use more than a single zero to indicate a *standard subdivision*, so that already existing zeros may be deleted until only a single zero remains.

For example, THE PHILOSOPHY OF EDUCATION entails the addition of —oi, the standard subdivision for PHILOSOPHY AND THEORY, to 370 EDUCATION, but the answer is 370.1—not 370.01. Only the single zero is needed to indicate the standard subdivision. Similarly, A HISTORY OF TECHNOLOGY, using 600 and 09, is not 600.09 but 609. You can check both these numbers in the schedules since DC prefabricates them to help the user.

Which of the following numbers is correct for
A HISTORY OF THE ZOOLOGICAL SCIENCES

599   turn to frame 42
590.9   turn to frame 52
590.09 turn to frame 60

58 No. You have made the same mistake twice

Remember that unless the scheme gives you a specific instruction (as it often does—you should always read the notes under the headings very carefully) then you need only *one* zero to show that you are using a standard subdivision.

Now go back to frame 57 and read the lesson carefully. Then try the question again.

---

59 You are wrong

You have added the correct area notation, but for some reason you have chosen to add an extra 9. It is true that in DC the digit 9 is traditionally associated with historical, and consequently also geographical treatment, but there is no need to do anything more than DC tells you. At 331.29 HISTORICAL AND GEOGRAPHICAL TREATMENT OF WAGES, for example, you are told simply to add the area notation. There is no necessity to do any more than this, so that the correct answer is 331.2944.

Now try this one
DESIGN IN SCANDINAVIA
745.449948   turn to frame 54
745.449—48 turn to frame 49
745.44948   turn to frame 55

You added—o9 to the class number without any alteration, which gives you a number with two zeros. But we said that except in very special circumstances *one* zero would be sufficient to indicate a *standard subdivision,* and if the original class number had a zero already (or even two) then we could take away the surplus zeros until there remains only the one that we need.

Now try again. Select a number for
ESSAYS ON ARCHITECTURE
720.08 turn to frame 58
728   turn to frame 42
720.8 turn to frame 52

You have read the instruction wrongly. The area notation is to be added directly to the specific number for HISTORICAL AND GEOGRAPHICAL TREATMENT. This means that the area notation is added to the 9 subdivision and not to the number for the class as a whole. The example of SCHOOL ENROLMENT IN RURAL AREAS should have not the answer 371.211734, but 371.2191734.

Now try another
INDUSTRIAL RELATIONS IN THE AFRO-ASIAN BLOC OF UNALIGNED COUNTRIES
331.09-17165 turn to frame 56
331.0917165 turn to frame 67
331.017165 turn to frame 64

62 No, you are wrong

In this class geographical subdivision is important enough to have several places allotted to it and these places end in the digits used already at the beginning of the area notation. Obviously then there is no need to use the same digits twice, or to continue to use the 9 that is often characteristic of geographical subdivision in DC. THE MORMON CHURCH uses 289.34-.39 for geographical subdivision and the 4-9 are the 4-9 of the area notation for various countries. When we add 42 for GREAT BRITAIN there is no need to repeat the 4 already in the class number and so the correct answer is 289.342. In any case DC always gives the base number to which you may add the subdivision notation.

Now try another example
NORWEGIAN PRINTS
769.94481 turn to frame 68
769.9481 turn to frame 70
769.981 turn to frame 66

---

63 No

Class numbers that have no instruction to add area notation directly can still be given geographical subdivision by using the *standard subdivision* —09 HISTORICAL AND GEOGRAPHICAL TREATMENT to introduce area notation. When you do this you have only to add —09 to the class number and then the correct area notation, but you do not need another 9.

The number for SILVICULTURE, for instance, is 634.95 which has no specific instruction to add the area notation, but if we add —09, then we can use the area notation —495 GREECE to make the class number 634.9509495.

Now try another
GOLD AND SILVER MINING IN SOUTH AMERICA
622.3420998 turn to frame 71
622.342098 turn to frame 69
622.3428 turn to frame 65

64 No. You have made the same mistake twice

Although you have answered one question on geographical subdivision correctly you probably do not understand the idea of it as clearly as you should. Table 2: AREAS includes both a list of countries (—3 to —9) and a list of physiographic features and regions (—1). All these subdivisions behave in just the same way, and are added under instruction to relevant class numbers.

Now turn back to frame 52 and read it again. Then answer the question, thinking about why you choose the answer you do, and continue the programme.

---

65 No

You have added the area notation directly to the class number although there is no instruction allowing you to do so. Where there is no instruction we have to use a standard subdivision to help us.

Now, although we are actually using two kinds of subdivision at once, the —09 of the standard subdivision HISTORICAL AND GEOGRAPHICAL TREATMENT has no real meaning here beyond showing that the next group of digits comes from the area notation to indicate geographical subdivision. This means that in effect we add —09 to any class number that does not already have an instruction to add area notation, and add the area notation after the —09.

MOTELS IN NEW YORK STATE
728.509747   turn to frame 69
728.5099747 turn to frame 63
728.5747   turn to frame 71

You have realised quite rightly that in a class like this geographical subdivision matters more than in many others and that DC therefore gives over a number of the subdivisions of the class for this purpose. This results in the omission of digits characteristic of this kind of division, like 9, and it usually means a shorter class number. But you have gone too far and left out too many digits. The intention of DC in assigning for example, 34-39 of 289 for the HISTORICAL AND GEO-GRAPHICAL TREATMENT OF THE MORMON CHURCH is to use the 4-9 of that class number as the 4-9 of the area notation. The 4 of 42 GREAT BRITAIN must be present in some form, whether we think of it as the 4 of 289.34 with the remaining 2 added, or 289.3 with 42 added. In any case DC always gives the base number to which you may add the subdivision notation.

Now try again
THE MUSIC OF FRANCE

781.744   turn to frame 70
781.7444   turn to frame 62
781.74   turn to frame 68

Sometimes not all the area tables are relevant for dividing a given class number and the instruction in DC may limit the area notation to be used. This sometimes looks a little confusing but it is just the same as the method we have seen already.

For example in 379 EDUCATION AND THE STATE geographical subdivision is put at the end as 379.4-.9 PUBLIC EDUCATION BY CONTINENT, COUNTRY (etc) with the instruction

Add area notations 4-9 from Table 2 to base number 379

in other words the 4-9 of 379.4-.9 *are already* the 4-9 of the area notation so that PUBLIC EDUCATION IN INDIA is 379.54.

In all cases of this kind with any table of subdivisions (and we shall meet this again later) DC always gives the *base number* to which the notation from the table of subdivisions should be added. Sometimes it is the class number you are concerned with. But sometimes it is a part of it, and if this is the case DC will always make it clear just what you are to do.

What is the number for

THE MORMON CHURCH IN GREAT BRITAIN

289.342   turn to frame 70
289.3942   turn to frame 62
289.32   turn to frame 66

68 No. You have now made the same mistake twice

There is no need to be confused by this use of area notation. It occurs when geographical subdivision is important in a class and when several subdivisions of the class can be given over to it, instead of confining it to only one. When this happens we usually find that the subdivision digits are the same as the digits beginning the area notation, so they can be omitted, and in such cases DC will give you the base number to which you may add the subdivision notation.

Now go back to frame 67 and read the explanation again carefully. Study the examples and try the question again.

---

69 Correct

Remember when you use this general kind of geographical subdivision that DC may have made arrangements for geographical subdivision in the class you have chosen, and you should read all instructions and notes very carefully. If there is a subdivision already allocated for historical and geographical treatment *you must use it* rather than use the —09 standard subdivision extended by area notation.

What is the number for
BIRDS OF ANTARCTICA
598.20989 turn to frame 72
598.2989   turn to frame 74

So far we have used area notation only on finding specific instructions in the schedules, but there are many numbers that may need geographical subdivision where no instruction is given at all. In cases like this we must return for a moment to the *standard subdivisions* and look at —09 HISTORICAL AND GEOGRAPHICAL TREATMENT. Although this is primarily a subdivision representing the historical approach to the treatment of a subject it can also introduce area notation to give geographical subdivision.

For instance 622 MINING has no special subdivision for historical or geographical treatment. A HISTORY OF MINING would thus naturally be 622.09 and since the standard subdivision —09 contains —093-099 with the instruction

Add 'Areas' notation 3-9 from Table 2 to base number —09

we can specify MINING IN SOUTH AFRICA.

This use of —09 to introduce an area table number will work for any class number in DC that does not already have a specific instruction about geographical subdivision.

Now try this one
SILVICULTURE IN GREECE
634.9509495   turn to frame 69
634.95099495 turn to frame 63
634.95495   turn to frame 65

71 No. You have just made the same mistake again

The use of area notation with any class number that does not have specific instruction for its use is really very simple. Add the standard subdivision —09 to the class number and add the area notation directly to that.

Now go back to frame 70 and read the explanation of the reasons for this again. Then study the examples and try the question again with these in mind.

---

72 No

You are using the 09 standard subdivision extended by area notation theoretically quite correctly, but in this class there is no need for it since DC has already provided places for regional treatment. In cases like this you must follow the instructions.

Now try again. What is the correct number for
PUBLIC EDUCATION IN WALES

379.209429 turn to frame 73
379.429   turn to frame 74

73 No

You are still trying to use the *standard subdivision* —09 and area notation when there is no need to do so. DC gives specific instruction and makes special arrangements in many classes for you to use area notation directly and you must always read all notes and instructions very carefully before you decide on your class number.

Now turn to frame 74 and continue with the programme.

---

74 Good

You will have noticed by now that the *standard subdivisions* also include 0901-0904 HISTORICAL PERIODS, on pp 2132-2133 of DC's index volume. Note that these are *general* historical periods only, for use when no country or locality is specified. You will learn later how to add period divisions to countries. For the time being remember that this list of period divisions is for use without specification of country.

These historical subdivisions must always be used as given; they cannot be abbreviated as area notation sometimes can. For example, THE WINDS OF THE WORLD IN THE NINETEENTH CENTURY uses 551.518 and the standard subdivision 09034 NINETEENTH CENTURY to give the class number 551.51809034.

Which of these numbers is correct for
WORLD COMMERCE 1950-1960
380.090945 turn to frame 78
380.09045   turn to frame 81

75 No

You are still using the whole of the standard subdivision as well as the —09 for HISTORICAL AND GEOGRAPHICAL TREATMENT. You must remember that the period divisions are themselves extensions of HISTORICAL TREATMENT and consequently already include 09 as part of the number.

Now go back to frame 74 and read the explanation again carefully and study the examples. Then try the question again, and read all the notes in DC as you work it.

---

76 Good

Note that as always DC gives the base number to which you should add the notation from the Languages Table. Occasionally (as we saw with 'Areas' notation) that base number is not quite the same as the class number you are concerned with. For example, in the same class as 039 ENCYCLOPEDIAS IN OTHER LANGUAGES you will see 034 ENCYCLOPEDIAS IN FRENCH, PROVENCAL, CATALAN, in which the instruction reads

Add 'Languages' notation 41-49 from Table 6 to base number 03.

Note that the base number is 03 and *not* 034. This is because the 4 already exists as part of the Languages notation. So a FRENCH LANGUAGE ENCYCLOPEDIA is a synthesis of 03 and -41 : 034.1

What is the correct number for
THE BIBLE IN DUTCH
220.53931   turn to frame 84
220.533931   turn to frame 79

77 No

You are still making the same mistake.

The number to which you should add the language notation is the *base* number, not the whole notation of the class you are concerned with (which already includes the first digit of the language notation).

Now go back to frame 76, and read the instruction and try the problem again.

---

78 No

You have used too many digits to introduce the historical period. The list on pp 2132-2133 of the index volume of DC is intended to be used in straightforward cases just like any other notation from the standard subdivisions. This means that the —09 that begins the period number is the 09 meaning HISTORICAL TREATMENT so that all you have to do is to add the period number to the class number in place of the —09 HISTORICAL AND GEOGRAPHICAL TREATMENT.

Now try again
PUBLIC EDUCATION IN THE SEVENTEENTH CENTURY
379.20909032 turn to frame 75
379.209032   turn to frame 95

Because the range of notation offered for extension by a language subdivision begins at 220.53 you have added the language number —3931 DUTCH directly to it. But DC gives you the base number 220.5 for the addition of language notation, because the 3 is already included in the subdivision number, and the answer is therefore

220.53931

Now try
SPANISH LANGUAGE SERIAL PUBLICATIONS
056.61 turn to frame 77
056.1   turn to frame 84

You are trying to include the dash from the language notation which is simply DC's way of showing that another number must be used as a base to which the language notation is added. Just join the two pieces of notation together, but leave out the dash.

Now try this one
TEACHING ROMANIAN IN ELEMENTARY SCHOOLS
372.65591 turn to frame 76
372.6591   turn to frame 87
372.65-591 turn to frame 82

Standard and geographical subdivision are not the only kinds of sub-division to have their own general tables in DC. This edition, DC 18, has introduced three others of a general kind: of *persons*, of *language* and of *racial, ethnic and national groups*. Like the standard and geo-graphical subdivisions, they can never be used alone, but must always be used with a number from the general or auxiliary schedules. Unlike the standard and geographical subdivisions they may be added *only* when the schedules give explicit permission and instruction. They are not used as frequently as the standard and geographical subdivisions, but you should know where to find them and how to use them.

First look at Table 6 LANGUAGES on pp 2580-2599 of volume 2 of DC. This gives a complete list of languages, and subdivisions from it may be used whenever you see an instruction to add LANGUAGES notation.

For example 372.3-372.8 SPECIFIC ELEMENTARY SCHOOL SUBJECTS includes 372.65 FOREIGN LANGUAGES with the instruction

Add ' Languages ' notation 1-9 from Table 6 to base number 372.65 so that FRENCH AS AN ELEMENTARY SCHOOL SUBJECT is the synthesis of 372.65 and —41 and produces 372.6541.

Now try one for yourself
AN ENCYCLOPEDIA IN LATVIAN
039-9193   turn to frame 80
039.9193   turn to frame 76
039.193   turn to frame 87

82 No, you are wrong again

You are still making what is really an elementary mistake. DC tells you exactly what to do; follow the instructions.

Now read 81 again and see if you can do better.

---

83 No, you are wrong

The 'Persons' notation should be added *as it stands* to the base number shown in DC's schedules. To insert o simply to mark off the subdivision notation is unnecessary and wrong.

Try another one
SEX INSTRUCTION FOR ADOLESCENTS
301.4180544 turn to frame 93
301.418544   turn to frame 91

84 You are quite right

A similar variation in applying subdivision notation occurs when the instruction tells you to use *some* but not all of the language notation. This is for the same reason as using a different base number: because only a limited range of languages is involved, and quite possibly some of the notation already exists.

For example 038 ENCYCLOPEDIAS IN SCANDINAVIAN LANGUAGES says

Add to 038 the numbers following 39 in 'Languages' notation 396-398 from Table 6 so that a SWEDISH LANGUAGE ENCYCLOPEDIA is formed from the synthesis of 038 and 7 (from 397) to give 038.7.

Remember that DC will always tell you the base number if it is different from the class you are concerned with, and will also tell you explicitly which pieces of notation to ignore and which to use.

Now go on to frame 85.

Now let us look at another table of subdivisions—Table 5: RACIAL, ETHNIC, NATIONAL GROUPS, on pp 2566-2579 in volume 2 of DC.

This notation is used in the same way as the language notation, but this time to indicate peoples. If you have been used to using earlier editions of DC and you are now finding out about DC18 you will notice that RACIAL, ETHNIC, NATIONAL GROUPS are used to specify people where earlier editions of DC had to use a kind of language subdivision. Do not confuse Table 5: RACIAL, ETHNIC, NATIONAL GROUPS in DC18 with Table 6: LANGUAGES.

For example, in the main class LIFE SCIENCES, 572 HUMAN RACES has a subclass 572.8 SPECIFIC RACES with the instruction

Add ' Racial, Ethnic, National Groups ' notation 0-9 from Table 5 to base number 572.8

so that a number for THE RACES OF EAST AND SOUTHEAST ASIA is formed from 572.8 and —95 to make 572.895.

What is the correct number for
SLAV RACIAL PSYCHOLOGY

155.84—918	turn to frame 92
155.84918	turn to frame 88
155.8418	turn to frame 89

---

86 No

You are still making the same mistake. DC's instructions are quite clear and you should follow them.

Go back to frame 85 and try again.

87 No

You have quite properly tried to add the language notation to the base number but because the last digit of the base number is the same as the first of the language notation you tried to suppress one of the repeated digits. This is quite wrong. DC tells you to add the language number as it stands.

Now try again
ALBANIAN PROVERBS
398.991991 turn to frame 76
398.91991 turn to frame 82

88

The last of these tables on pp 2600-2632 in volume 2 is Table 7: PERSONS, described by physical and mental characteristics, by social, sex or ethnic characteristics, and by their interests or occupations. Like the tables we have just seen, it may be used only on explicit instruction by DC.

For example 808.8992 LITERATURE FOR AND BY PERSONS OF SPECIFIC CLASSES includes the instruction

Add 'Persons' notation 09-79 from Table 7 to base number 808.8992

so that LITERATURE FOR AND BY HELMINTHOLOGISTS is formed from 808.8992 and —595 to make 808.8992595.

What is
CUSTOMS OF BLACKSMITHS
676.3904 turn to frame 90
390.4676 turn to frame 93
390.40676 turn to frame 83

89 No

You are committing the basic mistake of *including* the dash which is only DC's way of showing that this notation may not be used by itself. Always omit the dash when adding the subdivision notation.

Try another one
THE SEMITIC RACES
572.892   turn to frame 88
572.8—92 turn to frame 86

---

90 No

You have combined the elements of your number the wrong way round. The subdivision notation cannot stand by itself (or stand first in a compound number, for that matter) and it must always be added to a number from the main or auxiliary schedules. The correct number was

390.4676 CUSTOMS OF BLACKSMITHS

Now turn to frame 93.

91 No

You have over compensated for your previous mistake. Although you should not *insert* o when there is no need, you should leave a o in if there is one in the subdivision notation. If you still feel uncertain about the use of the 'Persons' notation from Table 7, go back to frame 88 and read the instruction again.

Otherwise turn to frame 93.

---

92 No

For some reason you have omitted the 9 of —918 SLAV RACES when adding the racial, ethnic, national groups notation to the base number 155.84. This is quite wrong. Add *all* of this notation to the number indicated in the schedules.

Now try again
CELTIC FOLK MUSIC
781.72916 turn to frame 88
781.7216   turn to frame 86

93 Good

You will have noticed that on the first page of Table 7 : PERSONS you are instructed to observe a *table of precedence*. We shall meet this again later. For now remember simply that if you have to decide between describing a FEMALE INFANT as FEMALE —042 or INFANT —0542 then you choose the higher in the table of precedence, in this case —0542 INFANT.

Now go on to frame 95.

---

94 Not quite

You have chosen both the right class number for the main subject and the right part of the list of general aspects that gives the sub-division you want, but you have not put them together according to the instructions. Always read notes and instructions very carefully and examine the examples.

Now try again
THE ARCHAEOLOGY OF THE PENTATEUCH

221.9302221 turn to frame 101
222.1093   turn to frame 96
222.193   turn to frame 98
222.1022193 turn to frame 103

So far we have learned how to add form or geographical subdivisions to an already satisfactory class number, but it is often possible to add on subdivisions of the subject itself that are not actually listed in that class. This is done according to an *add* instruction. This *add* device is used in several ways, but its purpose is really always the same: to economise on the size of the printed schedules and thus save the time and patience of the user in using them.

It is the same kind of thing in use as adding an area notation to a number under instruction, but instead of taking a number from a special table, you take it from a class where enough detail has already been worked out for your purpose.

Generally speaking there are three types of *add* device. A class can be extended by numbers taken from (a) the whole classification (b) another class within the same subject field (c) a similar class in another subject field.

Take (a) first. This is the easiest form of the device and it occurs usually when a class can be divided by any object or idea that exists. For example, in 704.94 SPECIFIC SUBJECTS IN ART, after a list of subjects frequently chosen by artists, DC includes a class for everything else, at 704.949, and says:

Add 001-999 to base number 704.949 [etc]
Thus the representation of AIRCRAFT (which is 629.133 in ENGINEERING) is 704.949629133.

Which of the following numbers represents
A SPECIAL LIBRARY ON NUMISMATICS
737.026 turn to frame 100
020.737 turn to frame 102
026.737 turn to frame 97

In nearly all these cases enough instruction and example is given in the schedules to make this type of *add* device almost as easy as the first type.

The third type of *add* device is the use of the detailed subdivision of a topic in one subject field for the same or a similar topic when it occurs in another field.

For instance, there is no need to list all the insect pests by name under 632.7 INSECT PESTS, since there is already a list of insects at 595.7 INSECTS in ZOOLOGY, and these may be used to extend 632.7:

Add to 632.6 the numbers following 59 in 592-599, *eg* SNAILS 632.643

Another example can be found in 634.9 FORESTRY
634.96 INJURIES, DISEASES, PESTS
Add to 634.96 the numbers following 632 in
632.1-632.9, *eg* FOREST FIRES 634.9618

Here the subdivisions of 632 PLANT INJURIES (in this case the original number was 632.18 FIRES) are attached to 634.96

INJURIES, DISEASES [etc]	634.96
FIRES (plant injuries)	632.18
FOREST FIRES	634.9618

Now try this one for yourself
ELECTROPLATING OF COPPER ALLOYS

673.31732   turn to frame 104
673.3732   turn to frame 108
671.73206733 turn to frame 111
673.3   turn to frame 105

The second type of *add* device is used mostly within a class, when its members are all or nearly all divided in the same way. In such a case DC gives a complete list of the subdivisions for one of the members or for the class in general and instructs the classifier to use them and their notation for any other member.

An example can be seen in 617 SURGERY where the subdivisions .01-.09 list general aspects that can be used with any of the particular kinds or applications of surgery listed in 617.1-617.9 that are *starred for an instruction to subdivide.

Another frequently encountered example occurs in HISTORY where each country is supplied with a set of *period subdivisions* which are common to all subdivisions of place within the country, extended by area notation. Thus in 942 GREAT BRITAIN the TUDOR period is given the number 05 so that

TUDOR ENGLAND is	942.05
LANCASHIRE IN THE TUDOR PERIOD is	942.7205
BUCKINGHAMSHIRE UNDER THE TUDORS is	942.57505

Which of these numbers is correct for
THE SYMBOLISM OF THE SONG OF SOLOMON

223.964   turn to frame 94
223.9064   turn to frame 96
220.6402239 turn to frame 101
223.9022064 turn to frame 103

98 No, you have made the same mistake again

Most classes that use this *add* device within their own fields have very clear and specific instructions on where the list of topics can be found that are used as subdivisions and how they are applied. Usually it is a matter of adding a few terminal digits of a general list to the subject subdivisions (*ie* the ordinary class numbers) in the class with which you are working.

Now go back to frame 97 and read the lesson carefully. Then try the question again.

---

99 No, you have made the same mistake twice

The *add* device, especially in the examples we have seen so far, is really quite simple. The class number you should be using has an instruction to Add 001-999 and all you have to do is to add the class number you want for the subject subdivision just as you added area notation when forming a geographical subdivision.

Now go back to frame 95 and read the lesson carefully. Then try the question again.

You have not looked carefully enough at your main class number. The heading (and number) that you have chosen is too general—and in any case there is *no* 'Add 001-999 ' instruction there!

You should have looked through the schedules of the class a little more carefully, and you would then have found a class reserved especially for this kind of division.

Always check the schedules to see if there is a class more appropriate than the one you first have in mind. Do not forget to use the summary at the beginning of the class if there is one.

SPECIAL LIBRARIES, for example, are given the class 026, to which we may add the number for the subject of the library; this saves any awkward additions to 020. A SPECIAL LIBRARY ON NUMISMATICS is therefore 026.737.

Now try
APTITUDE TESTS FOR MATHEMATICAL ABILITY
153.951   turn to frame 99
153.9451   turn to frame 97
510.15394 turn to frame 100

100 No

You have found the right numbers but you have put them together the wrong way round. This is probably because you did not read the *add* instructions carefully enough, if you read them at all.

In the example A SPECIAL LIBRARY ON NUMISMATICS it is 026 SPECIAL LIBRARIES that says 'add 001-999 to base number 026 [etc]' and it should be a simple matter to add 737 NUMISMATICS to it to get 026,737.

Now try another
IMPORT DUTIES ON PERFUMES
336.26666854   turn to frame 97
336.26466854   turn to frame 102
668.540336266 turn to frame 99

---

101 No

You have not understood the application of this kind of *add* device. Further you have mistaken what is only the subdivision for the main class and *vice versa*.

In the example THE SYMBOLISM OF THE SONG OF SOLOMON the main subject is THE SONG OF SOLOMON 223.9 and SYMBOLISM is the subdivision. SYMBOLISM is represented for all the books of the BIBLE by the 64 which represents it in DC's general list for the BIBLE: 220.64 SYMBOLISM AND TYPOLOGY. The note in the class number where the subdivisions are to be used always gives clear instructions and examples and these must always be read carefully.

Now try again
COMPLICATIONS OF HEART SURGERY
617.4121   turn to frame 94
617.41201   turn to frame 96
617.010617412 turn to frame 98
617.412061701 turn to frame 103

103 No

You have realised (quite correctly) that you must add to the class number a subdivision borrowed from the model list, but you have not realised that since this operates within the class there is no need to repeat the digits that reveal the borrowed number's origin.

In the example THE SYMBOLISM OF THE SONG OF SOLOMON only 64 needs to be taken from 220.64 SYMBOLISM OF THE BIBLE—the 22 represents the BIBLE of which THE SONG OF SOLOMON is a part. The correct answer for this reason is not 223.90220964 but 223.9064

Try this one
WEAVING COTTON
677.21066702824 turn to frame 98
677.212824   turn to frame 94
677.2124   turn to frame 96
677.02824066721 turn to frame 101

---

104 No

You have understood the instruction enough to realise that you must delete the unnecessary digits from the borrowed number, but you must be careful about the application of the rest.

Here you have probably misunderstood the example. However these instructions are phrased, in the type of *add* device we are considering here the application of the borrowed number is largely a matter of taking away the digits which represent the class from which it has been borrowed, leaving only the subdivision.

For instance, in FOREST FIRES we are really taking the subdivisions of 632, and so 632, the common element representing the original class, must be ignored.

Now try again
THE STATISTICS OF DEATH FROM PARATYPHOID
312.26   turn to frame 105
312.2669274 turn to frame 106
616.92743122 turn to frame 111
312.269274   turn to frame 108

You have not followed the *add* instruction.

This class is one which may be extended in detail by the application of subdivisions from another class. There are too many of these in the scheme for DC to itemise subdivisions every time, and this, as we have seen, is one way of keeping the printed scheme a manageable size.

There is no difficulty about the application of this kind of subdivision, if you remember the method we followed with the geographical subdivision built into one class number.

In the example FOREST FIRES the instruction at 634.96 INJURIES (etc) says:

Add to 634.96 the numbers following 632 in 632.1-632.9 *eg* FOREST FIRES 634.9618.

All you have to do is to compare this with the borrowed number for FIRES: 632.18. It is very easy to see from this that 632 has been ignored and only the 18 representing the subdivision FIRES has been added to the class concerned: 634.96 INJURIES (etc).

Try this one
THE WURTZ-FITTIG REACTION AS AN INDUSTRIAL CHEMICAL PROCESS

660.2844   turn to frame 106
660.284421   turn to frame 104
660.28441   turn to frame 108
547.21660284 turn to frame 111

106 No. You have made the same mistake twice.

This kind of *add* device is quite easy to use. All you have to do is to use the terminal or variable digits of the class number which supplies your subdivision. The constant digits of that original class are not needed and should be ignored.

Now go back to frame 96 and read the lesson carefully. Then try the question again.

---

107 No

You have not chosen the correct main class. What you have chosen is the main class originally containing the detailed subdivision. Remember THE MINERALOGY OF SAPPHIRES! You must always ensure that the class number you choose belongs to the correct general subject field.

What you should have done here was to use the subdivision you chose as an extension to the correct main class, where you would have found an instruction telling you to do exactly that.

Now return to frame 108, read the instructions carefully and work the example again.

A more complex form of this kind of *add* device occurs when not one but several subdivisions are reserved for extension by subdivisions from another class. The borrowed subdivisions are important so more than just one place of the borrowing class is made available to receive them. Again, the notation is shorter, but the application a little less easy to understand.

What DC does is to give a *base number* (we met this when dealing with area notation) derived from the range of notation in the class you are concerned with, and to include it in the usual kind of *add* instruction.

For example the naming of SPECIFIC FLOWERS in 635.9 FLORICULTURE is made possible by the reservation of the subclasses 635.933-.939 for parallel subdivision like 583-589. This might seem complicated were it not for DC's instruction:

Add to 635.93, the numbers following 58 in 583-589, *eg*, CACTUS 635.93347.

In other words, since the final digits 3-9 of 635.933-.939 are already present in 583-589, DC derives the base number 635.93 for a normal *add* device.

635.933-.939 FLOWERS BY FAMILY [etc]
635.93   [base number]
    583-589 FLOWERS (botany)
    583.47   CACTUS (botany)
635.93347   CACTUS (floriculture)

What is the number for
DYEING WILD SILK
667.392   turn to frame 114
667.3392   turn to frame 112
677.392   turn to frame 107
667.31392 turn to frame 116

109 No. You have made the same mistake twice

Although this kind of *add* device looks complex it is really no different from the kinds you have met already. All you need to do is to match the last digits of the main number you are using with the last digits of the borrowed number and see at what point you must begin to use them.

Now go back to frame 108 and read the lesson carefully. Then try the question again.

---

110 No, you are wrong

You have observed that DC instructs at the general heading '.001-.009 standard subdivisions' and you have continued to use the double zero even for subdivisions of 658. This is wrong. DC does do it on occasion, but when this happens there is always a very clear and specific instruction (look, for example, at 617 SURGERY AND RELATED TOPICS).

In cases of the kind we are now concerned with, however, DC has realised that there is no confusion in using the standard subdivision normally.

Now try again
PLANS OF NARROW GAUGE RAILWAYS
625.1020223 turn to frame 117
625.10200223 turn to frame 115

111 No

You have found the original class number for the specific subject and you have added to it the class number for the general field you are really concerned with. They are the wrong way round.

Always make sure that the class number you choose belongs to the correct subject field. (Remember THE MINERALOGY OF SAPPHIRES.)

If you had read the schedules carefully at the correct class you would have seen an instruction telling you to add the detailed subdivision from the class where it is originally listed.

In the example FOREST FIRES the instruction at 634.96 INJURIES (etc) says:

Add to 634.96 the numbers following 632 in 632.1-632.9 *eg* FOREST FIRES 634.9618.

All you have to do is to compare 632.9618 with the borrowed number for FIRES: 632.18. It is easy to see from this that 632 has been ignored and only the 18 representing the subdivision FIRES has been added to the class concerned: 634.96 INJURIES (etc).

Now try another

ANTHROPOMETRIC STUDIES OF THE HUMERUS
573.6   turn to frame 105
573.6717   turn to frame 108
611.71705736 turn to frame 106
573.611717   turn to frame 104

The form of the *add* device that you have just learned about is not difficult if you proceed slowly and think clearly. With it you have mastered the most complex form of the addition of single subdivisions that DC uses.

Sometimes it is necessary to use synthesis twice or even three times in the same class number. Generally speaking unless a note in the schedules invites you to do this it is better to limit synthesis to one addition, but there are some classes whose subject naturally requires more, and some occasions when almost any subject may need more.

We can divide multiple synthesis roughly into several kinds and we shall look at these one by one. They include:

The use of a standard subdivision after some other subdivision like an *add* device or area notation;

The use of physiographic features from Table 2: Areas with other area notations;

The use of two added subdivisions in a subject for the sake of difference or comparison;

The use of general aspects of a subject with other constructed divisions of that subject.

Remember, however, that except in cases involving *standard subdivisions* and *area notation* which can be used anywhere in DC, you should beware of trying too hard to link up subdivisions from the schedules unless DC instructs or permits you to do so.

Now turn to frame 113 and continue.

113 Very often you will want to add a standard subdivision to a class number in which you have already used another kind of subdivision.

Look at 391 COSTUME in the schedules. You will see there that, as we have noticed with other classes previously, DC instructs you to use 391.001-.009 for the standard subdivisions. This is because DC uses the subdivisions 391.01-.05 for COSTUMES OF SPECIFIC CLASSES OF PEOPLE with an *add* instruction for the detail. Clearly we could not then use 391.01-.05 for standard subdivisions or we should be using 391.022 for both ILLUSTRATIONS OF COSTUME (standard subdivision 022 means ILLUSTRATIONS) and COSTUMES OF ROYALTY. DC tells us therefore to use a *double* zero for standard subdivision, which serves to distinguish the two numbers

    391.022 COSTUMES OF ROYALTY

    391.0022 ILLUSTRATIONS OF COSTUME

This much we have learned already. What we need now is a way of using both *special* and *general* subdivisions together—to be able to say, for example, ILLUSTRATIONS OF COSTUMES OF ROYALTY.

In spite of the appearance of the instruction at 391 (and this is true of all such instructions) you do *not* have to use a double zero for standard subdivision within the class. Once 022 ROYALTY has been added to 391 there is no likelihood of mistaking a further *single* zero for anything but a standard subdivision. ILLUSTRATIONS can thus remain 022, to make 391.022022 ILLUSTRATIONS OF COSTUMES OF ROYALTY. The first 022 *must* mean ROYALTY according to the schedules, and the second (once the first kind of subdivision has been used) must be a standard subdivision.

Instructions to use *double* zeros apply *only* to the class numbers where they are given and *not* to any of their subdivisions. DC has worked out the effect of this and you are quite safe to use the standard subdivisions in the normal way. In any case where there might be confusion DC has an instruction telling you what to do and a list of the kinds of subdivision and how to apply them.

Now try one yourself
CASE STUDIES IN THE MANAGEMENT OF LARGE ENTERPRISES
658.023300186 turn to frame 110
658.02330186 turn to frame 117

114 No

You have contracted the borrowed number too far. You should always study the example given in the instruction very carefully, and compare it with the original class number from which the borrowed subdivision has been taken.

Now try
RUSSIAN SHORTHAND

653.4917   turn to frame 112
653.44917 turn to frame 116
653.417   turn to frame 109
491.7   turn to frame 107

---

115 No, you are still making the same mistake

A double zero is needed only for standard subdivisions of the heading because that heading also has special subdivisions that are introduced by a single zero, like 625.102 NARROW GAUGE RAILWAYS. If standard subdivisions were not given an extra zero then NARROW GAUGE RAILWAYS would be confused at 625.102 with MISCELLANEOUS FORMS OF PRESENTATION. But at any of the special subdivisions themselves there is no further subdivision that uses a zero other than a standard subdivision, so the normal practice can be adopted.

Now go back to frame 113 and read the explanation carefully. Then try the question again.

It is important always to study the example given in the *add* instruction in order to avoid including too many digits from the borrowed number (as you have done here) or removing too many. You should compare the example given in the instruction with the original class number from which the borrowed subdivision has been taken.

Now try again

MACHINERY IN THE ELECTRONICS INDUSTRY

621.38   turn to frame 107

338.4562138   turn to frame 112

338.45662138 turn to frame 109

338.45638   turn to frame 114

Another kind of double synthesis involves specifying both the place and the period of a subject. Earlier in the programme you used period divisions by themselves with simple class numbers. Quite often, however, you will have to use period divisions after you have used area notation, to specify time as well as place. This is quite easily done, as you will see if you read the instruction in DC at —3-9 SPECIFIC CONTINENTS, COUNTRIES [etc] in the index volume. There you will see among other instructions that 01-09 may be used *following a number from* Table 2 to give historical periods. The important point to notice here is that the historical periods are *not* taken from the *general* historical periods that you used before from the standard subdivisions, but are taken instead, like an ordinary *add* device, from the historical subdivisions of the individual country concerned in the HISTORY classes 930-999.

For example, in 946 HISTORY OF SPAIN the period subdivision for the MOORISH DYNASTIES is 02, so we may add this to the area notation —46 SPAIN as a general time-and-place subdivision for any subject to mean IN SPAIN UNDER THE MOORISH DYNASTIES.

Try one for yourself
RUSSIAN SCIENCE UNDER STALIN

509.4709042   turn to frame 125
509.470842   turn to frame 120
509.47090842 turn to frame 123

118 No. You have just made the same mistake twice.

This addition of a period subdivision to area notation is quite simple if you remember to take it from the country's own schedules in the main class HISTORY, and to add it using a single zero as an indicator.

Now turn back to frame 117 and read the explanation again carefully and the instruction in DC at —3-9 SPECIFIC CONTINENTS, COUNTRIES [etc]. Then try the question again.

---

119 No, you are still making the same mistake.

Return to frame 120 and read the instruction again. Follow DC's instructions when you work the problem and see if you can get the right answer this time.

Time and place are not the only kinds of subdivision that may be used together. It is possible sometimes to join RACIAL, ETHNIC, NATIONAL GROUPS and AREAS; or PERSONS and AREAS.

For example 301.4 SOCIAL STRUCTURE contains 301.451 AGGRE-GATES OF SPECIFIC NATIONAL, RACIAL, ETHNIC ORIGIN, divided by both RACIAL, ETHNIC, NATIONAL GROUPS and AREAS in 301.4512-.4519:

Add 'Racial, Ethnic, National Groups' notation 2-9 from Table 5 to base number 301.451, *eg* FRENCH NATIONALS 301.45141; then add 0 and to the result add 'Areas' notation 1-9 from Table 2, *eg* FRENCH NATIONALS IN THE UNITED STATES 301.45141073.

Note the use of the 0 to separate and signal the second subdivision.

What is the number for
EDUCATION OF GIPSIES IN GREAT BRITAIN
371.9791497042 turn to frame 127
371.9742091497 turn to frame 124
371.979149742   turn to frame 121

121 No, you chose the wrong number

You have followed DC's instructions quite properly in putting the 'Racial, Ethnic, National Groups' notation first, and the place second, but you omitted the o that DC uses as a separator and indicator.
Try another one

THE SOCIAL STRUCTURE OF ROMAN CATHOLICS IN NORTHERN IRELAND
301.42582416 turn to frame 119
301.42520416 turn to frame 127

---

122 No

The 'Areas' notation is correct in both cases, but you have combined the elements in the wrong order. DC specifically instructs you to put the country emphasised first, and the other country second. If in doubt you should in any case use the *earlier* notation first. Always follow DC's instructions.

Now turn to frame 128.

123 No

You are using the correct historical period number, taken from the schedules for the country in the main class HISTORY, but you have tried to use it in the same way that you used the *general* historical periods from the standard subdivisions. Those are for use only when no country or locality is specified and are not relevant at all here. When you use a period subdivision from a country's historical schedules all you have to do is to use a single zero as an indicator, as happens in most countries' historical schedules.

Now try again
DAMS AND RESERVOIRS IN REPUBLICAN ROME
627.8093702   turn to frame 120
627.809370902   turn to frame 118
627.8093709014 turn to frame 125

---

124 No, you are wrong

You have put the 'Areas' notation *before* the 'Racial Ethnic, National Groups' notation; DC tells you to do just the opposite. If your answer meant anything at all (and it doesn't) it might mean something like THE EDUCATION OF BRITONS IN GIPSY ENCAMPMENTS.

Try another example, and this time follow DC's instructions carefully.
THE SOCIAL STRUCTURE OF ROMAN CATHOLICS IN NORTHERN IRELAND
301.452841602 turn to frame 119
301.452820416 turn to frame 127

125 No

You are trying to use a number from the *general* historical periods given in the standard subdivisions. These can be used only when no country or locality is specified. If a country or locality is specified then period subdivisions must be taken from that country's schedules in the HISTORY main class, and added to the area notation with a single zero as indicator, as it is in nearly all countries.

Now try again
POSTAL COMMUNICATION IN EIGHTEENTH CENTURY EUROPE

383.0940253   turn to frame 120
383.094090253   turn to frame 123
383.09409033   turn to frame 118

---

126 No, this is the wrong answer

You have chosen a perfectly good number for PLOT IN SPANISH LITERATURE, but you have ignored the form and the period—both of them probably of greater significance. DC's instruction is first to choose the subdivision of *greatest significance* (the subdivision with fewest zeroes) and then to see if it may be subdivided further.

Now go back to frame 148 and try again.

Of course it is also possible in certain circumstances to combine two subdivisions of *the same kind* and DC will always give you appropriate instructions. As we have just seen with the combination of 'Racial, Ethnic, National Groups' and 'Areas' notations, a zero is used to separate and distinguish the second subdivision.

For example in 309 SOCIAL SITUATION AND CONDITIONS, the subclass 309.2233 INTERNATIONAL ASSISTANCE needs dividing both by the country assisting and by the country assisted. US ASSISTANCE to other countries is formed from 309.2233 and —73 from the 'Areas' notation to make 309.223373. Assistance to TANZANIA must then use —678 from the 'Areas' notation, prefaced by the indicator 0, to make 309.2233730678 US ASSISTANCE TO TANZANIA.

Find the correct number for
FOREIGN RELATIONS BETWEEN FRANCE AND CAMBODIA
327.440596 turn to frame 128
327.596044 turn to frame 122

Very occasionally you may find yourself using quite sophisticated combinations of notation. If for instance you wanted to find a number for THE EDUCATION OF IRAQI STUDENTS IN ENGLISH SPEAKING COUNTRIES you begin with 371.97 to which you add (as DC instructs) 927 for ARAB AND MALTESE, further divided by 'Area' notation 567 for IRAQ. After the separating 0 you add 175 REGIONS WHERE SPECIFIC LANGUAGES PREDOMINATE, extended by 'Languages' notation 21 for ENGLISH. The assembled number is thus

    371.97927567017521

You probably think this is far too complex and cumbersome a notation to use. And you would be right. It is very rare either to find a book on such a complex subject; special collections may include such documents, but you would probably not then use DC anyway. Moreover it is rare to find DC permitting such clumsy notation. As we shall see in a moment, DC prefers simplicity if possible and instructs you accordingly. We included this example just to show what can sometimes be done with the Tables of subdivisions.

Now turn to frame 129.

129 Two classes have special Tables of subdivision of their own. At one time these classes were fully enumerated, and had quite elaborate instructions to add sections of notation from one subclass to numbers in another subclass. But now they have been tidied up, and you may use the special subdivisions just as you have become used to using the general subdivisions like persons or areas or forms of presentation.

First look at the table for 400 LANGUAGE. It is Table 4: SUB-DIVISIONS OF INDIVIDUAL LANGUAGES, listing problems, aspects, tools etc. It is found on pp 2561-2565. This notation may be added to any starred item in 400 LANGUAGE—though not of course in any other class. Thus PORTUGUESE GRAMMAR combines 469 PORTUGUESE and —5 STRUCTURAL SYSTEM (GRAMMAR) from the special Table of sub-divisions, to make 469.5.

What is
A DICTIONARY OF STANDARD CZECHOSLOVAKIAN

491.863   turn to frame 137
491.8603   turn to frame 131
491.86   turn to frame 140

---

130 No, you are wrong

You are still making the same mistake. It is very simple to use the special Table of subdivisions. To the starred class number (or to the base number that DC gives you in doubtful cases) add the notation from Table 4.

Now go back to 129, read the instruction again, and try the problem once more.

131 No

You have assumed that the special subdivision notation needs a o to indicate its presence. This is not necessary, and indeed is contrary to the instructions in DC. The notation from Table 4 is to be added *directly* to the base number. Remember the example of PORTUGUESE GRAMMAR, that combined 469 and —5 to make 469.5.

Now try again
PRONUNCIATION OF UKRAINIAN

491.79152   turn to frame 137
491.79   turn to frame 140
491.790152   turn to frame 130

---

132 No

You have combined the numbers in the wrong order.

DC's general instruction on combining language numbers to describe bilingual dictionaries is to use the less known language number first, because dictionaries are customarily sought to translate from the less known language. If you are in doubt as to which is the less known language, then you should use first the notation that comes *later* in the schedules. Of course you may have good reasons, depending on your users or your stock, to vary that order. But here we have a normal situation, without special circumstances. So you should put the later number first, and then add the earlier number after the 3 that means DICTIONARIES.

Now try
A RUSSIAN/TURKISH DICTIONARY

491.739435   turn to frame 139
494.3539171 turn to frame 141

133 No, you have chosen the wrong number

Although it is true the 820 is ENGLISH LITERATURE, and that —08003 is correct notation for the ELIZABETHAN PERIOD, formed from —0800 base number for period and —3 ELIZABETHAN in the period table for ENGLISH LITERATURE, you did not notice that 82 is the base number for ENGLISH LITERATURE—*not* 820. The correct answer should have been

  820.08003 A COLLECTION OF ELIZABETHAN ENGLISH LITERATURE

Try another one
A COLLECTION OF EARLY MEDIEVAL GERMAN LITERATURE
830.08001   turn to frame 143
830.8001   turn to frame 135

---

134 No

You are making the mistake (which you have probably made before) of ignoring the base number that DC gives you in any class whose notation is not appropriate for the addition of a subdivision, so that your resulting number has too many zeroes.

Try again
A COLLECTION OF FRENCH LANGUAGE LITERATURE BY WRITERS OF THE AFRO-ASIAN BLOC
840.80917165   turn to frame 145
840.080917165   turn to frame 136
840.809017165   turn to frame 144

135 Correct

The rest of the —08 and —09 subdivisions for literature, respectively COLLECTIONS and GENERAL CRITICISM (etc), list features, elements, themes, and author/reader characteristics. For example —0913 IDEAL-ISM is a feature that may be added to a base number in the normal way to make 840.913 IDEALISM IN FRENCH LITERATURE.

Some of the notation —08 and —09 (which is more or less the same in both subdivisions) can be further extended by adding notation from appropriate tables, *eg* —098 LITERATURE FOR AND BY SPECIFIC RACIAL, ETHNIC, NATIONAL GROUPS, which has the instruction

Add 'Racial, Ethnic, National Groups' notation 01-99 from Table 5 to base number —098 [etc]

so that 820 ENGLISH LITERATURE (base number 82) may be extended by —098 which is itself extended by —96 NEGROES from Table 5 to make

820.9896 ENGLISH LANGUAGE LITERATURE BY NEGROES.

Now find a number for

A COLLECTION OF GERMAN LANGUAGE LITERATURE BY ENGINEERS

830.809262   turn to frame 145
830.0809262   turn to frame 134
830.80920962 turn to frame 144

---

136 No, you are wrong

You have made the same mistake twice, through not reading DC's instructions properly. The addition of subdivision notation is simple if you follow the instructions and read the examples carefully as you go.

Go back to frame 135 and read the explanation again carefully. Then try the problem once more.

137 Good

You probably noticed the instruction under —3 DICTIONARIES (etc) in Table 4; it offers a way to deal with BILINGUAL DICTIONARIES that is very useful, and of course frequently necessary. It is a synthesis similar to the synthesis you have met already in combining notations from the other tables of subdivisions.

SANSKRIT is 491.2; a SANSKRIT DICTIONARY is 491.23; a SANSKRIT/ENGLISH DICTIONARY adds —2 from Table 4 LANGUAGES to make 491.232.

It is usual to make the less familiar language the main number (since it is the less familiar language we probably want to translate)—but if there is any doubt we should use the language number that occurs *later* in the schedules as the main number.

Now try one for yourself
A BULGARIAN/FRENCH DICTIONARY

491.81341 turn to frame 141
491.41381 turn to frame 132

---

138 No, you are wrong

You have chosen a perfectly good number for SEVENTEENTH CENTURY SPANISH LITERATURE but you have ignored both NOVELLAS and PLOT. It could be that either or both may be used to extend 863.3 to be nearer what you want.

Go back to frame 148 and try again.

139 No

You are still making the same mistake. In situations where no particular interest is involved, the base number is the one for the *less known* language, or the one whose class number occurs *later* in the schedule. In this case the answer should have been

494.3539171 A RUSSIAN/TURKISH DICTIONARY

because 494.35 TURKISH occurs later in the schedules than 491.7.

Now go back to frame 137 and try again.

---

140 No

You have not added the notation from the subdivision at all. It is true that some numbers in 400 LANGUAGE cannot be extended by subdivision notation, but all of the starred places may be—and this was one of the starred places.

Try another one
ETYMOLOGY OF BRETON

491.68   turn to frame 130
491.6802 turn to frame 131
491.682   turn to frame 137

Another class that has its own special table of subdivisions is 800 LITERATURE: Table 3 SUBDIVISIONS OF INDIVIDUAL LITERATURES. At one time DC had many *add* instructions in this class and you would have had to consult the schedules in several places to find all the pieces of notation that might make up even as apparently simple a subject as REALISM IN FRENCH CLASSICAL DRAMA.

Now, however, the use of Table 3 for the 800 class makes it very easy. Remember that Table 3 may be used only with class 800, and never with any other, and its notation must be used with a starred number from the schedules—never alone. Note that in many cases (particularly of the major literatures) DC has carefully shown you the *base number* to use when adding notation from the special table.

The main part of the table is a complete list of features, forms and periods of literature, in various combinations; the last part is a brief indication of how to arrange criticism, biography and the works of single authors. We are concerned here with the first part.

Now have a look at the schedules at 840 LITERATURES OF ROMANCE LANGUAGES. FRENCH LITERATURE, and note that DC shows 84 as the base number. Then look for the table of subdivision so that you will be able to use it in the next few frames.

Now turn to frame 142.

142 Table 3: SUBDIVISIONS OF INDIVIDUAL LITERATURES contains four kinds of subdivision.

The first is the *standard subdivision* of the general kind, and DC indicates its position and notation, but for obvious reasons does not include any detail. —08 and —09, however, are not ordinary standard subdivisions; COLLECTIONS and HISTORY have special meanings in literature, and in DC's detailed working out of these we see the second and third kinds of subdivision for the first time. The second kind of subdivision is the *period* of literature. Here again DC cannot for obvious reasons list the periods; instead, each literature in the main schedules has its own list of periods and you are instructed to use the appropriate notation. FRENCH LITERATURE is 840 and in its period table at that class number 4 is the CLASSICAL PERIOD. In the table of subdivisions, —08 COLLECTIONS indicates periods —08001-08009 FROM SPECIFIC PERIODS by the instruction

Add to —0800 the notation from the period table for the specific literature, *eg* EARLIEST PERIOD —08001.

So A COLLECTION OF FRENCH LITERATURE OF THE CLASSICAL PERIOD is formed from the base number for FRENCH LITERATURE (84), the base number for COLLECTIONS BY PERIOD (—0800) and the notation from the French literature period table for the CLASSICAL period (4) to make 840.8004.

What is the number for
A COLLECTION OF ELIZABETHAN ENGLISH LITERATURE

820.08003   turn to frame 133
820.8003   turn to frame 135

143 No

You have made the same mistake twice. As with the standard subdivisions that you met earlier in this book you should eliminate unnecessary zeroes. Actually DC makes this easy for you, by telling you in 830 GERMAN LITERATURE that the base number to which you add subdivision notation is 83. This means that 83 and 08001 become 830.8001, because the decimal point always occurs after the third digit.

Now go back to frame 142 and try again.

---

144 No, you are wrong

You have too many zeroes. Although you have added the base number —0809 [COLLECTIONS FOR AND BY] PERSONS RESIDENT IN SPECIFIC REGIONS quite correctly, you have then added the extension to that notation *after another zero*. There is no need to do this, and in any case DC instructs you specifically to add further notation directly.

Try again
SPANISH LANGUAGE LITERATURE BY JEWS
860.8092296   turn to frame 145
860.08092296   turn to frame 134
860.80920296   turn to frame 136

145 Good, you are right

Now look at the rest of the Table 3: SUBDIVISIONS OF INDIVIDUAL
LITERATURES. From here on (—1-8) it is concerned chiefly with the
forms of literature, —1 POETRY, —2 DRAMA etc, to make

    821   ENGLISH POETRY

    895.11 CHINESE POETRY

Like —08 and —09, each subdivision may be divided by *features,
elements, themes* (division by period is rather different, as we shall see
in a moment).

Many of the literary form subdivisions —1-9, may also be divided
into *specific kinds eg* —102 DRAMATIC POETRY, —103 EPIC POETRY,
—106 DESCRIPTIVE (etc) to make

    821.02 ENGLISH DRAMATIC POETRY

Note, however, that *you may not combine* notations from —1008
(etc) and —102 (etc). If you wish to classify ROMANTICISM IN ENGLISH
DESCRIPTIVE POETRY you may *not* make up some number like
821.0600914, but you must include it without specification under
821.06.

Now turn to frame 146.

146 The major part of each of these subdivisions of literary form is division by period, using the appropriate notation from the period table of the literature you are concerned with. For example in —1 POETRY, —11-19 SPECIFIC PERIODS says

> Add to —1 the notation from the period table for the specific literature [etc]

So to 82 (base number) ENGLISH LITERATURE we add —1 POETRY (base number for period division) and 3 ELIZABETHAN PERIOD, to make

821.3 ELIZABETHAN POETRY

Before we go any further try one for yourself
SPANISH DRAMA OF THE GOLDEN AGE
862.3   turn to frame 148
862.13 turn to frame 150

---

147 No, you have the wrong answer

You did not read DC's instructions carefully enough and you are becoming confused. This time you have chosen to have too *few* 1's. 839.31 is DUTCH LITERATURE, so 839.311 is DUTCH POETRY. We know already that —1 divides directly by period, so that RENAISSANCE DUTCH POETRY must be 839.3112.

Now go back to frame 146, read the explanation again carefully and work the problem once more.

Unlike the other subdivision notations we have seen so far, the period subdivisions in literature may sometimes be subdivided further, by the addition of notation for features, elements, themes (etc) from Table 3. The notation that is added is anything following —10 in —1001-1009. For example we have already met —100914 ROMAN-TICISM, when we made up the number

821.00914 ROMANTICISM IN ENGLISH POETRY

Although we are *not* able to make up a number for ROMANTICISM IN ENGLISH DESCRIPTIVE POETRY we *can* make one up for ROMANTICISM IN ELIZABETHAN POETRY by adding the 0914 of —100914 to 821.3 ELIZABETHAN POETRY:

821.30914 ROMANTICISM IN ELIZABETHAN POETRY

Note, however, that you combine notation in this way only for collections and general works of criticism; *single* authors may not be treated in this way, but may either have everything by and about them collected together in the appropriate period, or simply at the appropriate form.

What is the correct number for
PLOT IN SEVENTEENTH CENTURY SPANISH NOVELLAS

863.00924	turn to frame 126
863.3	turn to frame 138
863.02	turn to frame 156
863.30924	turn to frame 151
863.30200924	turn to frame 153

149 No

You have ignored the table of precedence provided by DC at the head of the class. This table has been worked out so that you can place a compound subject in the most useful place. You have chosen what seems to you the most likely place, but it is not what DC wants you to do.

Now try another
THE PSYCHOLOGY OF FOSTER CHILDREN OF PRE-SCHOOL AGE
155.445 turn to frame 158
155.423 turn to frame 152

---

150 No, you are being careless

It is true that we used a —1 to introduce PERIODS in our example, but that was because —1 meant POETRY, for 821.3 ELIZABETHAN POETRY. In SPANISH DRAMA, the —2 means DRAMA, and it is subdivided directly by PERIOD, just like —1. So the correct answer is
862.3 SPANISH DRAMA OF THE GOLDEN AGE.

Try another one
DUTCH RENAISSANCE POETRY
839.3112 turn to frame 148
839.312 turn to frame 147

The need to choose between different features or aspects of a compound subject is well illustrated in 800 LITERATURE, where quite specific instruction is given. We have seen already in other classes that sometimes DC offers different kinds of division of the class that theoretically could appear in combination, but that DC wishes to be used singly. In cases of this kind DC usually gives a table of precedence or priorities. For example, in 155.4-.7 DEVELOPMENTAL PSYCHOLOGY there is a table showing various groupings. MALE INFANT TWINS could be placed variously at

155.422 INFANTS
155.432 BOYS
155.444 TWINS

but DC's precedence table at the top of the page compels us to use 155.444 TWINS. In the practical construction of the catalogue we could rely on the index to bring out the other aspects of the subject, but that is not our concern here.

Now choose a number for
FEMALE APPRENTICES AGED 16-18
331.55 turn to frame 149
331.34 turn to frame 158
331.4   turn to frame 154

152 No

You are still not reading and using the table of precedence correctly.

This is not different fundamentally from the many instructions that you see in DC that tell you to class operations on specific objects with the objects, and to ignore the operations.

Now go back to frame 151 and read the lesson again. Then try the question again, keeping the explanation and examples in mind.

---

153 No

You have made a valiant attempt at synthesis, but you have gone too far. You have assembled all the elements in what is theoretically the right order, and in what might be the right way. But DC does not want you to do this, in the interests of a simple, easily understood notation. So the instruction tells you to use period subdivision, and further divide that by literary feature—*and that is all.*

Now go back to 148 and try another answer

154 No

You have ignored the table of precedence provided by DC at the head of the class. This table has been worked out so that you can place a compound subject in the most useful place. You have chosen what seems to you the most likely place, but it is not what DC wants you to do.

Now try another
THE PSYCHOLOGY OF FOSTER CHILDREN OF PRE-SCHOOL AGE
155.445 turn to frame 158
155.423 turn to frame 152

---

155 No

You have chosen a heading which is only a part of the subject you should have in mind. A centred heading covers several subdivisions and is thus not a class number in itself; if you have a subject that can be described by the centred heading then you must use the next higher single class number.

Now try again
POTTERY
738.2-738.3 turn to frame 161
738   turn to frame 160
738.2   turn to frame 159

156 Wrong

You have chosen a perfectly good number for SPANISH NOVELLAS, but you have ignored both period and literary problems—and either *might* be used to extend the number you have chosen, and thus be a better description of PLOT IN SEVENTEENTH CENTURY SPANISH NOVELLAS.

Go back to frame 148 and try once more.

---

157 Quite right

Although DC usually shows a table of precedence to choose among different kinds of subdivision in a class, there are classes where no such table is given. There is at least, however, a summary of the kinds of subdivision, and you can use this if you are in doubt. What you should remember is that (just as you may have noticed in those classes where a precedence table was shown) the summary table should be used *backwards*: the most significant, or highest priority kind of subdivision usually appears at the bottom of the list. This is because the shelf order (the ordinary order of DC) is from general to specific, and what you are looking for is the most specific kind of subdivision because that is the most important.

For example, in the special literature table of subdivisions that we have just been using, the notation —0801—0809 is shown in outline in a summary, but no precedence table tells you what to choose if you have a subject like ROMANTICISM IN LITERATURE BY JEWS, where ROMANTICISM occurs in —0801 and LITERATURE BY JEWS in —0808. But because —0808 occurs *later* than —0801 you should choose that if you have no other special reason.

Now turn to frame 158.

158 The choice among different kinds of subdivision is symptomatic of DC's practical approach to classification and the provision of easily recognised and used labels for the subjects of books and the books themselves. Another feature of this kind in DC18 is the *centred heading* now used to give specific mention of general topics covering some, but not all, of the subdivisions of a general class.

Centred headings are particularly useful when a level of division would not normally be revealed by the addition of another digit in the class number, as when only a few of the ten places available for subdivision are used and the rest used for another principle of division.

For example in 470 ITALIC LANGUAGES. LATIN 471-476 are given over to CLASSICAL LATIN and 477-479 are used for other topics, like PRE- AND POST-CLASSICAL LATIN. 471-476 is therefore made a *centred heading* with the characteristic black stylised arrow head in the margin

►   471-476 Description and analysis of
standard classical Latin

Clearly a centred heading cannot give you a class number; by its nature it covers a group of numbers and serves only to define a subject area in the schedules. If the book you have to classify covers only one or two of the headings contained in the centred heading then you should use the first of the subordinate class numbers. But if the book you have to classify covers three or more of the headings contained in the centred heading then you must put it at the next higher single number.

In our example of 470 CLASSICAL LANGUAGES a book on CLASSICAL LATIN (centred heading 471-476) would take the class number 470; but a book on CLASSICAL LATIN GRAMMAR would take the number 475.

Now try this for yourself
EXTRACTIVE METALLURGY OF FERROUS AND NON-FERROUS METALS

669.1   turn to frame 155
669   turn to frame 160
669.1-669.7 turn to frame 161

159 No, you have just made the same mistake again

Centred headings were an innovation in DC17, but they do no more than rationalise a general principle. You have always had to use a more general number for a wide range of subordinate topics that could not find a specific class number, and that is precisely what you are being asked to do here.

Now go back to frame 158 and read the lesson carefully. Then try the question again.

---

160 Good, you are right

Sometimes DC does not wish you to use the next higher single class number for an area covered by a centred heading and then you will find an instruction telling you what to do. For example, the centred heading 172-179 APPLIED ETHICS instructs you to use 172.202 for comprehensive works, rather than 170. Take care always to read the notes and instructions to see if they help you in this way.

Now try
THE INSTRUMENTS OF THE STRING QUARTE1
787.1-787.4 turn to frame 161
787.01   turn to frame 163
787.1   turn to frame 155
787   turn to frame 162

161 No

A centred heading cannot provide you with a class number, since by its nature it covers several, but not all, of the ten subdivisions available to a class. DC does not allow you to say, for example 669.1-669.7 since this would be awkward to file. Instead you must use the next higher single number—in this case 669.

Now try
AIRCRAFT
623.741-623.746 turn to frame 159
623.74   turn to frame 160
623.741   turn to frame 155

---

162 No. You have done precisely what you were warned not to do.

787.1-787.4 has an instruction to use 787.01 for BOWED INSTRUMENTS IN GENERAL, rather than the general number 787.

Remember that DC always has an instruction telling you what number you should use instead of the range of notation at the centred heading.

Now go on to frame 163.

163 You have now worked through most of the kinds of problem that using DC might present. Always remember that the schedules give very clear examples and instructions, and in addition you will often find subjects in the index that appear in the schedules only in scope notes, or even that do not appear at all, but are the results of synthesis. In very difficult cases you may derive some extra help from your knowledge of classification theory, as you will see.

We learned very early that we could not always expect to find places in the classification scheme exactly equal to the subjects we were trying to classify. Indeed it was to solve some of these problems that we began to explore the possibilities of synthesis.

We must remember now that this situation, even with the help of synthesis, can still exist, and quite often we shall find complex subjects only some of whose ideas or aspects can be dealt with by the scheme. For example.

THE TRANSPORT OF VOTERS TO THE POLLS IN BRITISH ELECTIONS (which has, in fact, been the subject of a government publication) presents us with just such a problem. This specific topic does not exist in DC, and the nearest general heading is 324.242 VOTING PROCEDURE. GEOGRAPHICAL SUBDIVISION in this class, however, is given the special places 324.4-.9 because of its significance, so BRITISH ELECTIONS already has a number 324.42. These two numbers cannot be combined, and the user of the scheme must decide whether he wants his material in this field collected by the problems of SUFFRAGE AND ELECTIONS, regardless of country, or by COUNTRY, knowing that there is no way of arranging the material by PROBLEM under each country.

What we must do in such cases is to analyse the complex subject and recognise its constituent ideas and aspects. Then we must select the MOST IMPORTANT SUBDIVISIONS, as many as can be classified by the scheme, and ignore the others.

At one time DC had elaborate but ungainly arrangements to combine special subdivisions, common subdivisions and geographical subdivisions, but these have now been rejected by the editors, with a few exceptions. At this stage, authority in classifying passes out of the hands of the scheme into those of the classifier.

FROM NOW ON IT IS UP TO YOU

AN ALPHABETICAL INDEX TO THE EXAMPLES TO BE CLASSIFIED